Follow Me
A Scriptural Stations of the Cross Book

2nd Edition

"Do whatever he tells you." *John 2:5*

"Come, follow me." *Mark 10:21*

by Christine Haapala
Illustrated by Gus Muller

Suffering Servant Scriptorium
Fairfax, VA
www.sufferingservant.com

Nihil Obstat: Rev. Paul F. deLadurantaye, S.T.D.
Censor Librorum

Imprimatur: + Paul S. Lavorde
Bishop of Arlington
June 8, 2015

The *Nihil Obstat* and *Imprimatur* are official declarations that a book or pamphlet is free of doctrinal or moral error. No implication is contained therein that those who have granted the *Nihil Obstat* or *Imprimatur* agree with the contents, opinions, or statements expressed.

**Dedicated to
Immaculate Mary,
Mother of Sorrows**

**and In Memory of
Pope Saint John Paul II
1920 - 2005**

Special thanks to Father Michael Duesterhaus
for all his spiritual direction and encouragement.

In loving and prayerful memory of Gus Muller who died on May 25, 2015.
His spirit-filled watercolors in <u>Speak, Lord, I am Listening</u> and <u>Follow Me</u>
have enriched the spiritual life of so many.

Note from Publisher

In Christine and Gus' previous collaboration, the Catholic best-seller, <u>Speak, Lord, I am Listening</u>, they presented the Most Holy Rosary to the younger generation by making it clearer and more understandable through the richness of watercolors and the Word of God. Any devotion to Our Blessed Mother continues to her Divine Son, Jesus Christ. In this newest collaboration, inspired watercolors and profound selections of God's Word introduce children to the suffering of our Savior in a unique way as they walk each step with Him to Calvary.

In the Gospels, Jesus continually asks us to follow Him. One of the ways to follow Him is to join His Blessed Mother at the foot of the cross. In addition to beautiful watercolors and Sacred Scripture for each station, the collaborators, Gus and Christine, have included a selection from the homilies by Pope Saint John Paul II. They honor the late Pope by including with each station holy men and women he beatified or canonized. These saints epitomized self-sacrifice, and, primarily, lived and died in the last century. In this tribute, the collaborators wanted to emphasize the Pope's message to encourage all to strive for a life of holiness. The Pope's example of tireless worldwide evangelization, devout prayer life through a special devotion to the Blessed Virgin Mary, and serene acceptance of God's will in his final days of suffering is certainly a testament to his own holiness and sanctity.

In addition to the fourteen Stations of the Cross, the collaborators have included three other events: the Last Supper, the Resurrection, and the Holy Sacrifice of the Mass. The Stations of the Cross are not isolated events, but are a significant part of the Paschal Mystery and a pivotal event at the beginning of the One, Holy, Catholic, and Apostolic Church.

Christine and Gus recommend several different uses of this prayer book.

- For a group or community of people, use it during Stations of the Cross devotions. Have different leaders pray the Scriptures, prayers, and homily selections. Additionally, sing the opening response prayers with music found on page 37.
- For Catholic educators, use it as a textbook to teach The Stations of the Cross and a unit study on the Saints in Our Time.
- For individual reflection, use before or after Mass or during Eucharistic Adoration to walk the *Via Dolorosa*.
- For religious education of those too young to read, introduce this devotion, perhaps one Station at a time. Non-readers can appreciate the pictures, while parents read the Sacred Scripture and pray with them.

In this second edition, several significant events have occurred which we have incorporated. First, four of the people featured in the first edition have been canonized: Pope Saint John Paul II, Pope Saint John XXIII, Saint Jeanne Jugan, and Saint Kateri Tekakwitha. We have updated the language mentioning these saints and included selections of the canonization homilies. Second, pages 34-37 feature the changes in the Papacy over the last several years – with two new Popes – Benedict XVI and Francis, canonizations of John XXIII and John Paul II, and the beatification of Paul VI. Praise God for these wonderful new saints.

We hope that this book will increase devotion to this ancient tradition. May God bless you and may His mother bring you to her Son's cross where you can lay all your burdens down.

To Jesus through Mary,
Publisher
Suffering Servant Scriptorium

Table of Contents

Letter to Parents

My Dear Parents,

The fundamental truth of Jesus Christ, most especially His salvific offering of His life, is at the heart of the Stations of the Cross. The truth of Christ is owed to children. Having children walk along side Jesus, with the saints as guides to the path of life, should be at the heart of their life of Faith.

Many members of the Church are not truly familiar with the devotion of the Stations of the Cross. You may know of the devotion, but are not comfortable with this prayer. Or maybe you know and love making the Stations of the Cross, but do not know how to inculcate this love in your children.

Though especially encouraged during the Lent, the Stations of the Cross are not restricted to this season of preparation for Easter. This prayer can be done as a congregation, as a family, or as an individual. This book was written with two goals: for your children to know what they are praying and also that they would come to know those who have gone before them in the life of the Church. Sanctity is not solely the property of ancient times, but rather is the reality of the Church today and every day. The saints shown within the text demonstrate not only that holiness should be desired, but also that it is being attained - in our present age!

There are no assurances in raising children, but practices begun in youth can develop and deepen throughout life. Remember our Lord's instruction (rf. Mt 13:23), so if we plan on our children reaping the fullness of the Faith, the seeds need to be planted now, while they are still young.

Pray for your children. Pray WITH your children. And pray that your children not only know of their Savior, but that they know and love Jesus Himself.

In Christ, Through Mary,
Fr. Michael R. Duesterhaus
Priest of the Diocese of Arlington

Follow Me
A Scriptural Stations of the Cross Book

2nd Edition

"Do whatever he tells you."   *John 2:5*

"Come, follow me."   *Mark 10:21*

Jesus Christ proclaimed "I am the bread of life." *John 6:35*
At the Paschal table on Holy Thursday evening,
Jesus offered His Apostles Blessed Bread
and thus instituted a new Sacrament at

The Last Supper

Jesus took his place at table with the apostles. ... Then he took the bread, said the blessing, ... "This is my body, which will be given for you; do this in memory of me."

Luke 22:14, Luke 22:19

And while they were eating, he said, "… one of you will betray me."
… Then, after singing a hymn, they went out to the Mount of Olives.

Matthew 26:21,30

The Stations of the Cross

STATION I
Jesus is Condemned to Death

✝ We adore You, O Lord Jesus Christ, and we praise You.

✝ Because by Your holy cross You have redeemed the world.

"Are you the Messiah the son of the Blessed One?" Then Jesus answered, "I am." ... After Pilate had Jesus scourged, he handed him over to be crucified. ... Weaving a crown out of thorns, they placed it on his head. ... Live in love, as Christ loved us and handed himself over for us.

Mark 14:61-62, Matthew 27:26,29,

Mark 15:18, Ephesians 5:2

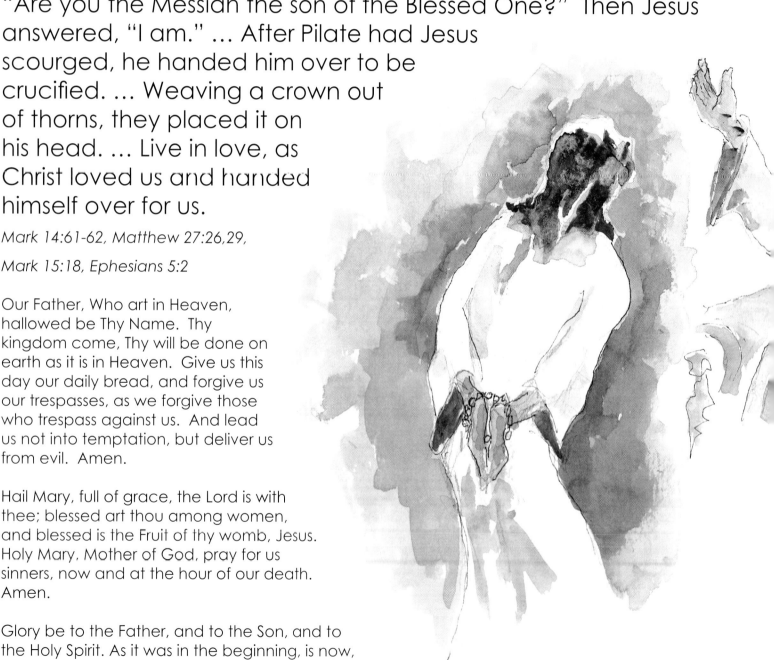

Our Father, Who art in Heaven, hallowed be Thy Name. Thy kingdom come, Thy will be done on earth as it is in Heaven. Give us this day our daily bread, and forgive us our trespasses, as we forgive those who trespass against us. And lead us not into temptation, but deliver us from evil. Amen.

Hail Mary, full of grace, the Lord is with thee; blessed art thou among women, and blessed is the Fruit of thy womb, Jesus. Holy Mary, Mother of God, pray for us sinners, now and at the hour of our death. Amen.

Glory be to the Father, and to the Son, and to the Holy Spirit. As it was in the beginning, is now, and ever shall be, world without end. Amen.

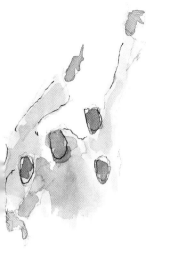

Faith, hope, love remain, these three; but the greatest of these is love. ... Your every act should be done with love. *1 Corinthians 13:13, 1 Corinthians 16:14*

Saint Gianna,
pray for us.

"Gianna Beretta Molla ... wrote: 'Love is the most beautiful sentiment the Lord has put into the soul of men and women'. ... Following the example of Christ, who 'having loved his own... loved them to the end', this holy mother of a family remained heroically faithful to the commitment she made on the day of her marriage. The extreme sacrifice she sealed with her life testifies that only those who have the courage to give of themselves totally to God and to others are able to fulfill themselves."

Homily of Pope Saint John Paul II at the Canonization of
Gianna Beretta Molla, May 16, 2004,
Saint Peter's Square, Vatican City

Station II
Jesus Carries His Cross

✝ We adore You, O Lord Jesus Christ, and we praise You.

✝ Because by Your holy cross You have redeemed the world.

"Crucify him, crucify him!" … We are … struck down, but not destroyed. … Oppressed and condemned, he was taken away. … Now two others, both criminals, were led away with him. … "Behold, I come to do your will, O God." … Now is the day of salvation.

John 19:6, 2 Corinthians 4:8-9,

Isaiah 53:8, Luke 23:32,

Hebrews 10:7, 2 Corinthians 6:2

Our Father, Who art in Heaven, hallowed be Thy Name. Thy kingdom come, Thy will be done on earth as it is in Heaven. Give us this day our daily bread, and forgive us our trespasses, as we forgive those who trespass against us. And lead us not into temptation, but deliver us from evil. Amen.

Hail Mary, full of grace, the Lord is with thee; blessed art thou among women, and blessed is the Fruit of thy womb, Jesus. Holy Mary, Mother of God, pray for us sinners, now and at the hour of our death. Amen.

Glory be to the Father, and to the Son, and to the Holy Spirit. As it was in the beginning, is now, and ever shall be, world without end. Amen.

"Everyone who listens to these words of mine and acts on them will be like a wise man who built his house on rock." ... The rock was the Christ.

Matthew 7:24, 1 Corinthians 10:4

Blessed Junipero Serra,
pray for us.

"Junipero Serra was a shining example of Christian virtue and the missionary spirit. ... Relying on the divine power of the message he proclaimed, Father Serra led the native peoples to Christ. ... He sought to further their authentic human development on the basis of their new-found faith as persons created and redeemed by God. He also had to admonish the powerful, ... not to abuse and exploit the poor and the weak."

Homily of Pope Saint John Paul II at the Beatification of
Father Junipero Serra, September 25, 1988,
Saint Peter's Square, Vatican City

Blessed Junipero Serra is to be canonized by His Holiness Pope Francis during a Papal visit to the United States at the Basilica of the National Shrine of the Immaculate Conception in Washington, D.C., September, 2015.

Station III
Jesus Falls the First Time

✝ We adore You, O Lord Jesus Christ, and we praise You.

✝ Because by Your holy cross You have redeemed the world.

The snares of death lay in wait for me. ... What strength have I that I should endure...? ... "Whoever wishes to come after me must deny himself, take up his cross, and follow me." ... Does he not see my ways, and number all my steps? ... "I am the way and the truth and the life." *Psalm 18:6, Job 6:11, Matthew 16:24, Job 31:4, John 14:6*

Our Father, Who art in Heaven, hallowed be Thy Name. Thy kingdom come, Thy will be done on earth as it is in Heaven. Give us this day our daily bread, and forgive us our trespasses, as we forgive those who trespass against us. And lead us not into temptation, but deliver us from evil. Amen.

Hail Mary, full of grace, the Lord is with thee; blessed art thou among women, and blessed is the Fruit of thy womb, Jesus. Holy Mary, Mother of God, pray for us sinners, now and at the hour of our death. Amen.

Glory be to the Father, and to the Son, and to the Holy Spirit. As it was in the beginning, is now, and ever shall be, world without end. Amen.

Jesus said, "Let the children come to me, ... for the kingdom of heaven belongs to such as these." ... "Whoever does not accept the kingdom of God like a child will not enter it." *Matthew 19:14, Mark 10:15*

Blessed Jacinta and Blessed Francisco, pray for us.

"Francisco was motivated by one desire - so expressive of how children think – 'to console Jesus and make him happy'. ... Francisco had a great desire to atone for the offences of sinners by striving to be good and by offering his sacrifices and prayers. The life of Jacinta, his younger sister by almost two years, was motivated by these same sentiments. ... Man's final goal is heaven, his true home, where the heavenly Father awaits everyone with his merciful love. ... Our Lady needs you all to console Jesus, who is sad because of the bad things done to him; he needs your prayers and your sacrifices for sinners."

Homily of Pope Saint John Paul II at the Beatifications of
Jacinta and Francisco Marto, May 13, 2000,
Fátima, Portugal

STATION IV
Jesus Meets His Afflicted Mother

✝ We adore You, O Lord Jesus Christ, and we praise You.

✝ Because by Your holy cross You have redeemed the world.

For God so loved the world that he gave his only Son. … Is he not the carpenter, the son of Mary? … Of her was born Jesus who is called the Messiah. … He will save his people from their sins. … Mary said: "My soul proclaims the greatness of the Lord; my spirit rejoices in God my savior." *John 3:16, Mark 6:3, Matthew 1:16,21, Luke 1:46-47*

Our Father, Who art in Heaven, hallowed be Thy Name. Thy kingdom come, Thy will be done on earth as it is in Heaven. Give us this day our daily bread, and forgive us our trespasses, as we forgive those who trespass against us. And lead us not into temptation, but deliver us from evil. Amen.

Hail Mary, full of grace, the Lord is with thee; blessed art thou among women, and blessed is the fruit of thy womb, Jesus. Holy Mary, Mother of God, pray for us sinners, now and at the hour of our death. Amen.

Glory be to the Father, and to the Son, and to the Holy Spirit. As it was in the beginning, is now, and ever shall be, world without end. Amen.

"Behold, your mother." ... A great sign appeared in the sky, a woman clothed with the sun, with the moon under her feet, and on her head a crown of twelve stars. *John 19:27, Revelation 12:1*

Saint Juan Diego,
pray for us.

"Happy Juan Diego, true and faithful man! ... Bless families, strengthen spouses in their marriage, sustain the efforts of parents to give their children a Christian upbringing. ... Show us the way that leads to the 'Dark Virgin' of Tepeyac, that she may receive us in the depths of her heart, for she is the loving, compassionate Mother who guides us to the true God."

Homily of Pope Saint John Paul II at the Canonization of
Juan Diego Cuauhtlatoatzin, July 31, 2002,
at the Basilica of Our Lady of Guadalupe, Mexico City, Mexico

11

STATION V
Simon Helps Jesus Carry His Cross

✝ We adore You, O Lord Jesus Christ, and we praise You.

✝ Because by Your holy cross You have redeemed the world.

"I have given you a model to follow, so that as I have done for you, you should also do." ... Bear one another's burdens, and so you will fulfill the law of Christ. ... They pressed into service ... Simon, a Cyrenian ... to carry his cross. ... You will then not have to bear it by yourself. *John 13:15, Galatians 6:2, Mark 15:21, Numbers 11:17*

Our Father, Who art in Heaven, hallowed be Thy Name. Thy kingdom come, Thy will be done on earth as it is in Heaven. Give us this day our daily bread, and forgive us our trespasses, as we forgive those who trespass against us. And lead us not into temptation, but deliver us from evil. Amen.

Hail Mary, full of grace, the Lord is with thee; blessed art thou among women, and blessed is the Fruit of thy womb, Jesus. Holy Mary, Mother of God, pray for us sinners, now and at the hour of our death. Amen.

Glory be to the Father, and to the Son, and to the Holy Spirit. As it was in the beginning, is now, and ever shall be, world without end. Amen.

12

God is love. ... The way we came to know love was that he laid down his life for us; so we ought to lay down our lives for our brothers.   *1 John 4:8,*
1 John 3:16

Blessed Teresa of Calcutta,
pray for us.

"Mother Teresa had chosen to be not just the least but to be the servant of the least. ... The cry of Jesus on the Cross ... had become the sole aim of Mother Teresa's existence and the inner force that drew her out of herself and made her 'run in haste' across the globe to labor for the salvation and the sanctification of the poorest of the poor. ... It was to Jesus himself, hidden under the distressing disguise of the poorest of the poor, that her service was directed."

Homily of Pope Saint John Paul II at the Beatification of
Mother Teresa of Calcutta, October 19, 2003,
Saint Peter's Square, Vatican City

Station VI
Veronica Wipes the Face of Jesus

✝ We adore You, O Lord Jesus Christ, and we praise You.

✝ Because by Your holy cross You have redeemed the world.

They spat in his face and struck him, while some slapped him. …
A bruised reed … My face I did not shield from buffets
and spitting. … "Come," says my heart, "seek
God's face"; your face, LORD, do I
seek! *Matthew 26:67, Isaiah 42:3, 50:6, Psalm 27:8*

Our Father, Who art in Heaven, hallowed be Thy Name. Thy kingdom come, Thy will be done on earth as it is in Heaven. Give us this day our daily bread, and forgive us our trespasses, as we forgive those who trespass against us. And lead us not into temptation, but deliver us from evil. Amen.

Hail Mary, full of grace, the Lord is with thee; blessed art thou among women, and blessed is the Fruit of thy womb, Jesus. Holy Mary, Mother of God, pray for us sinners, now and at the hour of our death. Amen.

Glory be to the Father, and to the Son, and to the Holy Spirit. As it was in the beginning, is now, and ever shall be, world without end. Amen.

It was not you who chose me, but I who chose you and appointed you to go and bear fruit that will remain. *John 15:16*

Saint Josephine Bahkita,
pray for us.

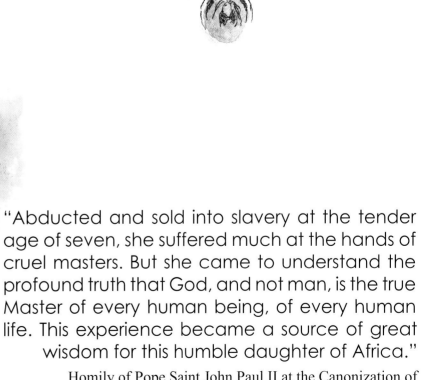

"Abducted and sold into slavery at the tender age of seven, she suffered much at the hands of cruel masters. But she came to understand the profound truth that God, and not man, is the true Master of every human being, of every human life. This experience became a source of great wisdom for this humble daughter of Africa."

Homily of Pope Saint John Paul II at the Canonization of Sister Josephine Bahkita, October 1, 2000, Saint Peter's Square, Vatican City

Station VII
Jesus Falls the Second Time

☦ We adore You, O Lord Jesus Christ, and we praise You.

☦ Because by Your holy cross You have redeemed the world.

Have pity on me, LORD, for I am weak; heal me, LORD, for my bones are trembling. ... "Whoever wishes to come after me must deny himself, take up his cross, and follow me." ... Whoever walks without blame, doing what is right, ... shall never be shaken. *Psalm 6:3, Mark 8:34, Psalm 15:2,5*

Our Father, Who art in Heaven, hallowed be Thy Name. Thy kingdom come, Thy will be done on earth as it is in Heaven. Give us this day our daily bread, and forgive us our trespasses, as we forgive those who trespass against us. And lead us not into temptation, but deliver us from evil. Amen.

Hail Mary, full of grace, the Lord is with thee; blessed art thou among women, and blessed is the Fruit of thy womb, Jesus. Holy Mary, Mother of God, pray for us sinners, now and at the hour of our death. Amen.

Glory be to the Father, and to the Son, and to the Holy Spirit. As it was in the beginning, is now, and ever shall be, world without end. Amen.

"Blessed are the poor in spirit..." ... For this momentary light affliction is producing for us an eternal weight of glory beyond all comparison.

Matthew 5:3, 2 Corinthians 4:17

Saint Jeanne Jugan,
pray for us.

"Sister Jeanne Jugan invites us to live the Gospel beatitude of poverty. ... She invites us especially to open our heart to the elderly, so often neglected and set aside. In proclaiming this woman Blessed, the Church intends to emphasize the charism of service rendered to the aged ... and love all people advanced in age."

Homily of Pope Saint John Paul II at the Beatification of
Sister Jeanne Jugan, October 3, 1982,
Saint Peter's Square, Vatican City

"Jeanne Jugan was concerned with the dignity of her brothers and sisters in humanity whom age had made more vulnerable, recognizing in them the Person of Christ himself. ... Jeanne lived the mystery of love, peacefully accepting obscurity and self-emptying until her death. Her charism is ever timely while so many elderly people are suffering from numerous forms of poverty and solitude and are sometimes also abandoned by their families. In the Beatitudes Jeanne Jugan found the source of the spirit of hospitality and fraternal love, founded on unlimited trust in Providence, which illuminated her whole life."

Homily of Pope Emeritus Benedict XVI at the Canonization of
Blessed Jeanne Jugan, October 11, 2009,
Vatican Basilica, Vatican City

Station VIII
Jesus Speaks to the Holy Women

✞ We adore You, O Lord Jesus Christ, and we praise You.

✞ Because by Your holy cross You have redeemed the world.

A large crowd of people followed Jesus, including many women who mourned and lamented him. Jesus turned to them and said, "Daughters of Jerusalem..." ... "Do not weep. The lion of the tribe of Judah, the root of David, has triumphed." ... "Today is holy to the LORD your God. Do not be sad, and do not weep." *Luke 23:27-28, Revelation 5:5, Nehemiah 8:9*

Our Father, Who art in Heaven, hallowed be Thy Name. Thy kingdom come, Thy will be done on earth as it is in Heaven. Give us this day our daily bread, and forgive us our trespasses, as we forgive those who trespass against us. And lead us not into temptation, but deliver us from evil. Amen.

Hail Mary, full of grace, the Lord is with thee; blessed art thou among women, and blessed is the Fruit of thy womb, Jesus. Holy Mary, Mother of God, pray for us sinners, now and at the hour of our death. Amen

Glory be to the Father, and to the Son, and to the Holy Spirit. As it was in the beginning, is now, and ever shall be, world without end. Amen.

"We have given up everything and followed you." ... "If you wish to be perfect, go, sell what you have and give to the poor, and you will have treasure in heaven. Then come, follow me." *Mark 10:28, Matthew 19:21*

Saint Katharine Drexel, pray for us.

"Mother Katharine Drexel was born into wealth. ... But from her parents she learned that her family's possessions were not for them alone but were meant to be shared with the less fortunate. ... She began to devote her fortune to missionary and educational work among the poorest members of society. Later, she understood that more was needed. With great courage and confidence in God's grace, she chose to give not just her fortune but her whole life totally to the Lord. ... May her example help young people in particular to appreciate that no greater treasure can be found in this world than in following Christ with an undivided heart and in using generously the gifts we have received for the service of others."

Homily of Pope Saint John Paul II at the Canonization of Mother Katharine Drexel, October 1, 2000, Saint Peter's Square, Vatican City

STATION IX
Jesus Falls the Third Time

✝ We adore You, O Lord Jesus Christ, and we praise You.

✝ Because by Your holy cross You have redeemed the world.

Make firm the knees that are weak ... Be strong, fear not! ... The just man falls seven times and rises again. ... "If anyone wishes to come after me, he must deny himself and take up his cross daily and follow me." ... The LORD, your God, shall you follow ... serving him and holding fast to him alone. *Isaiah 35:3-4, Proverbs 24:16, Luke 9:23, Deuteronomy 13:5*

Our Father, Who art in Heaven, hallowed be Thy Name. Thy kingdom come, Thy will be done on earth as it is in Heaven. Give us this day our daily bread, and forgive us our trespasses, as we forgive those who trespass against us. And lead us not into temptation, but deliver us from evil. Amen.

Hail Mary, full of grace, the Lord is with thee; blessed art thou among women, and blessed is the Fruit of thy womb, Jesus. Holy Mary, Mother of God, pray for us sinners, now and at the hour of our death. Amen.

Glory be to the Father, and to the Son, and to the Holy Spirit. As it was in the beginning, is now, and ever shall be, world without end. Amen.

"Not everyone who says to me, 'Lord, Lord,' will enter the kingdom of heaven, but only the one who does the will of my Father in heaven." *Matthew 7:21*

Saint Josemaría Escrivá, pray for us.

"Saint Josemaría spread in society the consciousness that we are all called to holiness whatever our race, class, society or age. In the first place, struggle to be saints yourselves, cultivating an evangelical style of humility and service, abandonment to Providence and of constant listening to the voice of the Spirit. In this way, you will be the 'salt of the earth' and 'your light so shine before men, that they may see your good works and give glory to your Father who is in heaven.'"

Homily of Pope Saint John Paul II at the Canonization of Father Josemaría Escrivá, October 6, 2002, Saint Peter's Square, Vatican City

Station X
Jesus is Stripped of His Garments

✝ We adore You, O Lord Jesus Christ, and we praise You.

✝ Because by Your holy cross You have redeemed the world.

They knelt before him in homage … they stripped him of the purple cloak. … They took his clothes and divided them into four shares, a share for each soldier. … They stare at me and gloat; they divide my garments among them; for my clothing they cast lots.

Mark 15:19-20, John 19:23,

Psalm 22:18-19

Our Father, Who art in Heaven, hallowed be Thy Name. Thy kingdom come, Thy will be done on earth as it is in Heaven. Give us this day our daily bread, and forgive us our trespasses, as we forgive those who trespass against us. And lead us not into temptation, but deliver us from evil. Amen.

Hail Mary, full of grace, the Lord is with thee; blessed art thou among women, and blessed is the Fruit of thy womb, Jesus. Holy Mary, Mother of God, pray for us sinners, now and at the hour of our death. Amen.

Glory be to the Father, and to the Son, and to the Holy Spirit. As it was in the beginning, is now, and ever shall be, world without end. Amen.

Stay awake, for you know neither the day nor the hour. ... Whoever serves me must follow me, and where I am, there also will my servant be.

Matthew 25:13, John 12:26

Saint Kateri Tekakwitha, pray for us.

"Kateri Tekakwitha, the 'Lily of the Mohawks', the Iroquois maiden ... is a kind, gentle and hardworking person, spending her time working, praying, and meditating. ... Even when following her tribe in the hunting seasons, she continues her devotions, before a rough cross carved by herself in the forest. ... The last months of her life are an ever clearer manifestation of her solid faith, straight-forward humility, calm resignation and radiant joy, even in the midst of terrible sufferings. Her last words, simple and sublime, whispered at the moment of her death, sum up, like a noble hymn, a life of purest charity: 'Jesus, I love you'".

Homily of Pope Saint John Paul II at the Beatification of
Kateri Tekakwitha, June 22, 1980,
Saint Peter's Square, Vatican City

"Leading a simple life, Kateri remained faithful to her love for Jesus, to prayer and to daily Mass. Her greatest wish was to know and to do what pleased God. She lived a life radiant with faith and purity. Kateri impresses us by the action of grace in her life in spite of the absence of external help and by the courage of her vocation, so unusual in her culture. In her, faith and culture enrich each other!"

Homily of Pope Emeritus Benedict XVI at the Canonization of
Blessed Kateri Tekakwitha, October 21, 2012,
Saint Peter's Square, Vatican City

STATION XI
Jesus is Nailed to the Cross

✝ We adore You, O Lord Jesus Christ, and we praise You.

✝ Because by Your holy cross You have redeemed the world.

Christ came as high priest … "This cup is the new covenant in my blood, which will be shed for you." … Golgotha. There they crucified him. … The message of the cross is … the power of God. … God is love. … God sent his only Son into the world so that we might have life through him. *Hebrews 9:11, Luke 22:20, John 19:17-18, 1 Corinthians 1:18, 1 John 4:8-9*

Our Father, Who art in Heaven, hallowed be Thy Name. Thy kingdom come, Thy will be done on earth as it is in Heaven. Give us this day our daily bread, and forgive us our trespasses, as we forgive those who trespass against us. And lead us not into temptation, but deliver us from evil. Amen.

Hail Mary, full of grace, the Lord is with thee; blessed art thou among women, and blessed is the Fruit of thy womb, Jesus. Holy Mary, Mother of God, pray for us sinners, now and at the hour of our death. Amen.

Glory be to the Father, and to the Son, and to the Holy Spirit. As it was in the beginning, is now, and ever shall be, world without end. Amen.

A man of suffering ... he was pierced for our offenses ... by his stripes we were healed. ... I have been crucified with Christ; yet I live, no longer I, but Christ lives in me.

Isaiah 53:3,5, Galatians 2:19-20

Saint Pio of Pietrelcina, pray for us.

"Our time needs to rediscover the value of the Cross in order to open the heart to hope. ... In God's plan, the Cross constitutes the true instrument of salvation for the whole of humanity and the way clearly offered by the Lord to those who wish to follow him. The Holy Franciscan ... wrote: 'In order to succeed in reaching our ultimate end we must follow the divine Head, who does not wish to lead the chosen soul on any way other than the one he followed ... the Cross' ... Is it not, precisely, the 'glory of the Cross' that shines above all in Padre Pio?"

Homily of Pope Saint John Paul II at the Canonization of Padre Pio (Father Pio of Pietrelcina), June 16, 2002, Saint Peter's Square, Vatican City

Station XII
Jesus Dies on the Cross

✠ We adore You, O Lord Jesus Christ, and we praise You.

✠ Because by Your holy cross You have redeemed the world.

From noon onward, darkness came over the whole land until three ... Jesus cried out again in a loud voice, and gave up his spirit. ... The earth quaked. ... "Truly, this was the Son of God." ... One soldier thrust his lance into his side, and immediately blood and water flowed out. ... He is expiation for our sins, and ... those of the whole world.

Matthew 27:45,50,51,54, John 19:34, 1 John 2:2

Our Father, Who art in Heaven, hallowed be Thy Name. Thy kingdom come, Thy will be done on earth as it is in Heaven. Give us this day our daily bread, and forgive us our trespasses, as we forgive those who trespass against us. And lead us not into temptation, but deliver us from evil. Amen.

Hail Mary, full of grace, the Lord is with thee; blessed art Thou among women, and blessed is the Fruit of thy womb, Jesus. Holy Mary, Mother of God, pray for us sinners, now and at the hour of our death. Amen.

Glory be to the Father, and to the Son, and to the Holy Spirit. As it was in the beginning, is now, and ever shall be, world without end. Amen.

Have mercy on me, God, … in you I place my trust. … in you I trust, I do not fear. *Psalm 56:2,4-5*

Saint Faustina, pray for us.

"Sister Faustina wrote: 'I feel tremendous pain when I see the sufferings of my neighbors. … I would like all their sorrows to fall upon me.' This is the degree of compassion to which love leads, when it takes the love of God as its measure! … It is this love which must inspire humanity today … to defend the dignity of every human person. Thus the message of divine mercy is also implicitly a message about the value of every human being. Each person is precious in God's eyes; Christ gave his life for each one. … Those rays from his heart touch them and shine upon them, warm them, show them the way and fill them with hope."

Homily of Pope Saint John Paul II at the Canonization of Sister Maria Faustina Kowalska, April 30, 2000, Saint Peter's Square, Vatican City

Station XIII
Jesus is Taken Down from the Cross

✝ We adore You, O Lord Jesus Christ, and we praise You.

✝ Because by Your holy cross You have redeemed the world.

He humbled himself, becoming obedient to death, even death on a cross. … God proves his love for us … Christ died for us. … By his wounds you have been healed. … Joseph of Arimathea went to Pilate and asked for the body of Jesus. … Thanks be to God who gives us the victory through our Lord Jesus Christ. *Philippians 2:8, Romans 5:8, 1 Peter 2:24, Luke 23:52, 1 Corinthians 15:57*

Our Father, Who art in Heaven, hallowed be Thy Name. Thy kingdom come, Thy will be done on earth as it is in Heaven. Give us this day our daily bread, and forgive us our trespasses, as we forgive those who trespass against us. And lead us not into temptation, but deliver us from evil. Amen.

Hail Mary, full of grace, the Lord is with thee; blessed art thou among women, and blessed is the Fruit of thy womb, Jesus. Holy Mary, Mother of God, pray for us sinners, now and at the hour of our death. Amen.

Glory be to the Father, and to the Son, and to the Holy Spirit. As it was in the beginning, is now, and ever shall be, world without end. Amen.

I rejoice in my sufferings for your sake, and in my flesh I am filling up what is lacking in the afflictions of Christ on behalf of his body, which is the church.

Colossians 1:24

Blessed Anne Catherine Emmerich, pray for us.

"Blessed Anne Catherine Emmerich told of 'the sorrowful passion of our Lord Jesus Christ' and lived it in her body ... a work of divine grace. Her material poverty contrasted with her rich interior life. ... She found this strength in the Most Holy Eucharist. Her example opened the hearts of poor and rich alike. ... Still today, she passes on to all the saving message: Through the wounds of Christ we have been healed."

Homily of Pope Saint John Paul II at the Beatification of Sister Anne Catherine Emmerich, October 3, 2004, Saint Peter's Square, Vatican City

Station XIV
Jesus is Laid in the Sepulcher

✝ We adore You, O Lord Jesus Christ, and we praise You.

✝ Because by Your holy cross You have redeemed the world.

Taking the body, Joseph wrapped it in clean linen and laid it in his new tomb. ... "They will kill him, but on the third day he will arise." ... I will turn their mourning into joy. ... Mary of Magdala came to the tomb ... and saw the stone removed from the tomb. *Matthew 27:59-60, Luke 18:33, Jeremiah 31:13, John 20:1*

Our Father, Who art in Heaven, hallowed be Thy Name. Thy kingdom come, Thy will be done on earth as it is in Heaven. Give us this day our daily bread, and forgive us our trespasses, as we forgive those who trespass against us. And lead us not into temptation, but deliver us from evil. Amen.

Hail Mary, full of grace, the Lord is with thee; blessed art thou among women, and blessed is the Fruit of thy womb, Jesus. Holy Mary, Mother of God, pray for us sinners, now and at the hour of our death. Amen.

Glory be to the Father, and to the Son, and to the Holy Spirit. As it was in the beginning, is now, and ever shall be, world without end. Amen.

No one has greater love than this, to lay down one's life for one's friends. ... Whoever seeks to preserve his life will lose it, but whoever loses it will save it. *John 15:13, Luke 17:33*

Saint Maximilian Kolbe, pray for us.

"All this happened in the concentration camp at Auschwitz. When the camp commander ordered the prisoners destined to die of starvation to fall in line, ... Father Maximilian Kolbe ... declared he was ready to go to death in the man's place, because the man was the father of a family and his life was necessary for his dear ones. ... Through the death of Father Maximilian Kolbe, a shining sign of this love was renewed in our century. ... The inspiration of his whole life was the Immaculata. ... In the mystery of the Immaculate Conception there revealed itself before the eyes of his soul that marvelous and supernatural world of God's grace offered to man."

Homily of Pope Saint John Paul II at the Canonization of Father Maximilian Maria Kolbe, October 10, 1982, Saint Peter's Square, Vatican City

"Amen, amen, I say to you, unless a grain of wheat falls to the ground and dies, it remains just a grain of wheat; but if it dies, it produces much fruit." *John 12:24*

The Resurrection

The LORD lives! Blessed be my rock! ... "I am the resurrection and the life." ... Mary of Magdala ... announced to the disciples, "I have seen the Lord." *Psalm 18:47, John 11:25, John 20:18*

Two of them were going to ... Emmaus. ... Then the two recounted what had taken place on the way and how Jesus was made known to them in the breaking of the bread. *Luke 24:13,35*

I will appoint one shepherd over them to pasture them. ... You are Peter, and upon this rock I will build my church, and the gates of the netherworld shall not prevail against it. *Ezekiel 34:23, Matthew 16:18*

Pope Blessed Pius IX, Pope Saint John XXIII, Pope Blessed Paul VI, and Pope Saint John Paul II, pray for us.

"Pope Pius IX's lengthy pontificate was not at all easy and he had much to suffer in fulfilling his mission of service to the Gospel. He was much loved, but also hated and slandered. ... During his moments of trial Pius IX found support in Mary, to whom he was very devoted. In proclaiming the dogma of the Immaculate Conception, he reminded everyone that in the storms of human life the light of Christ shines brightly in the Blessed Virgin."

"Pope Saint John's smiling face and two outstretched arms embracing the whole world. How many people were won over by his simplicity of heart. ... He called the Second Vatican Ecumenical Council, thereby turning a new page in the Church's history. ... The Council was a truly prophetic insight of this elderly Pontiff who, even amid many difficulties, opened a season of hope for Christians and for humanity."

Homily of Pope Saint John Paul II at the Beatifications of Popes Pius IX and John XXIII, September 3, 2000, Saint Peter's Square, Vatican City

"When we look to this great Pope, this courageous Christian, this tireless apostle, we cannot but say in the sight of God a word as simple as it is heartfelt and important: thanks! ... In this humility the grandeur of Blessed Paul VI shines forth: before the advent of a secularized and hostile society, he could hold fast, with farsightedness and wisdom – and at times alone – to the helm of the barque of Peter, while never losing his joy and his trust in the Lord."

Holy Mass for the conclusion of the extraordinary Synod on the family and Beatification of the Servant of God the Supreme Pontiff Paul VI, October 19, 2014, Saint Peter's Square, Vatican City

"This is also the image of the Church which the Second Vatican Council set before us. John XXIII and John Paul II cooperated with the Holy Spirit in renewing and updating the Church in keeping with her pristine features, those features which the saints have given her throughout the centuries."

Homily of Pope Francis at the Canonization of Blesseds John XXIII and John Paul II, April 27, 2014 (Divine Mercy Sunday), Saint Peter's Square, Vatican City

Christ's message of Divine Mercy and Love by His Passion and Death on the cross is re-presented daily in the Sacrament of the Eucharist at

The Holy Sacrifice of the Mass

Christ came as high priest ... he entered once for all into the sanctuary ... with his own blood, thus obtaining eternal redemption. Hebrews 9:11-12

"This is my body, which will be given for you." ... "This cup is the new covenant in my blood, which will be shed for you." ... "My Father gives you the true bread from heaven." ... "Whoever eats this bread will live forever." Luke 22:19-20, John 6:32, John 6:58

Pope Saint John Paul II died during the evening of April, 2, 2005, shortly after attending the Vigil Mass of the Feast of the Divine Mercy. Following his death, the Cardinals convened to elect a new Pope. By the grace of God, Cardinal Joseph Ratzinger was elected the next Pope on April 19, 2005. He took the name Benedict XVI.

Pope Emeritus Benedict XVI stepped down from his Papal chair on February 23, 2013. A new pope, Cardinal Jorge Mario Bergoglio from Argentina, was elected on March 13, 2013. In all humility, he took the name Francis in honor of St. Francis of Assisi.

They devoted themselves to the teaching of the apostles and ... the breaking of the bread and to the prayers. ... "Do this in remembrance of me." ... For as often as you eat the bread and drink the cup, you proclaim the death of the Lord until he comes.

Acts of the Apostles 2:42, 1 Corinthians 11:24,26

"Go into the world and proclaim the gospel." ... "Whoever listens to you listens to me. Whoever rejects you rejects me. And whoever rejects me rejects the one who sent me." Mark 16:15, Luke 10:16

"You know that it was the duty of the Conclave to give Rome a Bishop. It seems that my brother Cardinals have gone to the ends of the earth to get one. ... I would like to offer a prayer for our Bishop Emeritus, Benedict XVI. Let us pray together for him, that the Lord may bless him and that Our Lady may keep him. Now I will give the Blessing to you and to the whole world, to all men and women of good will."

Apostolic Blessing "Urbi et orbi,"
First Greeting of the Holy Father Pope Francis, March 13, 2013,
Central Loggia of St. Peter's Basilica, Vatican City

"When we journey without the Cross, when we build without the Cross, when we profess Christ without the Cross, we are not disciples of the Lord, we are worldly. My wish is that all of us, after these days of grace, will have the courage, yes, the courage, to walk in the presence of the Lord, with the Lord's Cross; to build the Church on the Lord's blood which was poured out on the Cross; and to profess the one glory: Christ crucified. And in this way, the Church will go forward."

Homily of Pope Francis at the Opening of
The Extraordinary Synod on the Family, October 5, 2014,
Vatican Basilica, Vatican City

Praying the Chaplet of Divine Mercy

(from Diary, Saint Maria Faustina Kowalska, <u>Divine Mercy in My Soul</u>, 476)

On the beads of a Rosary, begin with these opening prayers:

Our Father, Who art in Heaven, hallowed be Thy Name. Thy kingdom come, Thy will be done on earth as it is in Heaven. Give us this day our daily bread, and forgive us our trespasses, as we forgive those who trespass against us. And lead us not into temptation, but deliver us from evil. Amen.

Hail Mary, full of grace, the Lord is with thee; blessed art thou among women, and blessed is the Fruit of thy womb, Jesus. Holy Mary, Mother of God, pray for us sinners, now and at the hour of our death. Amen.

I believe in God, the Father almighty, Creator of heaven and earth, and in Jesus Christ, his only Son, our Lord, who was conceived by the Holy Spirit, born of the Virgin Mary, suffered under Pontius Pilate, was crucified, died and was buried; he descended into hell; on the third day he rose again from the dead; he ascended into heaven, and is seated at the right hand of God the Father almighty; from there he will come to judge the living and the dead. I believe in the Holy Spirit, the holy catholic Church, the communion of saints, the forgiveness of sins, the resurrection of the body, and life everlasting. Amen.

Pray on the Our Father bead:

Eternal Father, I offer You the Body and Blood, Soul and Divinity of Your dearly beloved Son, Our Lord Jesus Christ, in atonement for our sins and those of the whole world.

Repeat this prayer ten times on the decade of Hail Mary beads:

For the sake of His sorrowful Passion, have mercy on us and on the whole world.

Repeat these two sequences five times.

Conclude the Chaplet of Divine Mercy by praying this Doxology three times:

Holy God, Holy Mighty One, Holy Immortal One, have mercy on us and on the whole world.

"Saint John XXIII and Saint John Paul II were two men of courage, filled with the parrhesia of the Holy Spirit, and they bore witness before the Church and the world to God's goodness and mercy. They were priests, and bishops and popes of the twentieth century. They lived through the tragic events of that century, but they were not overwhelmed by them. For them, God was more powerful; faith was more powerful - faith in Jesus Christ the Redeemer of man and the Lord of history; the mercy of God, shown by those five wounds, was more powerful; and more powerful too was the closeness of Mary our Mother."

Homily of His Holiness Pope Francis at the Canonization of
Blesseds John XXIII and John Paul II, April 27, 2014 *(Divine Mercy Sunday)*,
Saint Peter's Square, Vatican City

Study Matrix

	Station	Gospel Reference	Virtues	Holy Person who Followed Jesus	Feast Day/ Memorial
I	Jesus is Condemned to Death	Matthew 27:1-2, 22-30 Mark 15:1-19 Luke 23:1-25 John 19:1-16	Generosity, Courage, Patience, and Love	Saint Gianna Beretta Molla	April 28
II	Jesus Carries His Cross	Matthew 27:31 Mark 15:20 John 19:16-17	Discipline, Industriousness, and Determination	Blessed Junipero Serra	July 1
III	Jesus Falls the First Time		Innocence, Modesty, and Cheerfulness	Blessed Jacinta Marto Blessed Francisco Marto	February 20
IV	Jesus Meets His Afflicted Mother		Fidelity and Truth	Saint Juan Diego Cuauhtlatoatzin	December 9
V	Simon Helps Jesus Carry His Cross	Matthew 27:32 Mark 15:21 Luke 23:26	Peace, Simplicity, and Compassion	Blessed Teresa of Calcutta	September 5
VI	Veronica Wipes the Face of Jesus		Justice	Saint Josephine Bakhita	February 8
VII	Jesus Falls the Second Time		Humility, Frugality, Forgiveness, Compassion, and Prudence	Saint Jeanne Jugan	August 30
VIII	Jesus Speaks to the Holy Women	Luke 23:27-31	Generosity and Gratitude	Saint Katharine Drexel	March 3
IX	Jesus Falls the Third Time		Diligence and Obedience	Saint Josemaría Escrivá de Balaguer	June 26
X	Jesus is Stripped of His Garments	Matthew 27:35 Mark 15:24 Luke 23:34 John 19:23-24	Gentleness, Hope, and Purity	Saint Kateri Tekakwitha	July 14
XI	Jesus is Nailed to the Cross	Matthew 27:37-49 Mark 15:25-36 Luke 24:33, 35-42 John 19:18-22, 25-29	Perseverance and Sacrifice	Saint Pio of Pietrelcina (Padre Pio)	September 23
XII	Jesus Dies on the Cross	Matthew 27:50-54 Mark 15:37-39 Luke 23:44-49 John 19:30	Long-Suffering, Love, Trust, and Piety	Saint Maria Faustina Kowalska	October 5
XIII	Jesus is Taken Down from the Cross	Matthew 27:57-59 Mark 15:42-45 Luke 24:50-52 John 19:38-39	Devotion	Blessed Anne Catherine Emmerich	February 9
XIV	Jesus is Laid in the Sepulcher	Matthew 27:59-61 Mark 15:46-47 Luke 23:53-55 John 19:41-42	Self Abandonment to Divine Providence, Martyrdom, and Courage	Saint Maximilian Maria Kolbe	August 14
Resurrection		Matthew 28:1-10 Mark 16:1-8 Luke 24:1-12 John 20:1-18	Faith, Hope, and Love	Pope Blessed Pius IX Pope Saint John XXIII Pope Blessed Paul VI Pope Saint John Paul II	February 7 October 11 September 26 October 22

Study Matrix

Dates Holy Person Lived	Examples of Other Holy People who Followed Jesus
Born: October 4, 1922, Magenta, Italy *Died:* April 28, 1962, Monza Maternity Hospital, Italy	Saint Anne, Saint Catherine of Sweden, Saint Peregrine, Saint Gerard Majella, Saint Monica
Born: November 24, 1713, Island of Majorca (Spain) *Died:* August 28, 1784, Mission San Carlos, Carmel, California	Saint Ignatius of Loyola, Saint Francis Xavier, Saint Boniface, Saint Patrick
Born: March 11, 1910, Portugal *Died:* February 20, 1920, Portugal *Born:* June 11, 1908, Aljustrel, Portugal *Died:* April 4, 1919, Aljustrel, Portugal	Saint Agnes, Saint Therese of Lisieux, Saint Dominic Savio, Saint Maria Goretti, Saint Aloysius Gonzaga, Saint John Bosco, Saint John Berchmans
Born: 1474, Tlayacac in Cuauhtitlan (near Mexico City, Mexico) *Died:* May 30, 1548	Saint Bernadette
Born: August 26, 1910, Skopje, Macedonia *Died:* September 5, 1997, Calcutta, India	Blessed Damien of Molokai, Saint Anthony of Padua
Born: 1868, Darfur, Sudan *Died:* February 8, 1947, Italy	Saint Martin de Porres, Saint Zita, Saint Peter Claver, Saint Martha
Born: October 25, 1792, Brittany, France *Died:* August 29, 1879, Pern, France	Saint Vincent de Paul, Saint Martin of Tours, Saint Elizabeth of Hungary
Born: November 26, 1858, Philadephia, Pennsylvania *Died:* March 3, 1955, Bensalem, Pennsylvnia	Saint Louis IX, King of France, Blessed Emilie Tavernier Gamelin, Saint Aloysius Gonzaga, Saint Frances of Rome
Born: January 9, 1902, Barbastro, Spain *Died:* June 26, 1975, Rome, Italy	Saint Dominic, Saint Benedict, Saint Teresa of Avila, Saint John of the Cross, Saint Aloysius Gonzaga, Saint Frances of Rome
Born: 1656, Auriesville, New York *Died:* April 17, 1680, Caughnawaga, Canada	Saint Isaac Jogues, Saint Helena
Born: May 25, 1887, Pietrelcina, Italy *Died:* September 23, 1968, San Giovanni Rotondo, Italy	Saint Paul, Saint Francis of Assisi, Saint Gertrude, Saint Catherine of Siena, Saint Rita of Cassia
Born: August 25, 1905, Glogowiec, Poland *Died:* October 5, 1938, Krakow, Poland	Blessed Margaret Mary Alacoque, Saint Margaret Clitherow, Saint Dismas, Saint Mary Magdalene
Born: September 8, 1774, Westphalia, Germany *Died:* February 9, 1824, Dulmen, Germany	Saints Matthew, Mark, Luke and John, Saint Francis de Sales, Saint Thomas Aquinas, Saint Augustine, Saint Bridget of Sweden, Saint Jerome
Born: January 7, 1894, Poland *Died:* August 14, 1941, Auschwitz Concentration Camp, near Krakow, Poland	Saint Agatha, Saint Charles Lwanga, Saint Victor of Marseilles, Saint Joseph of Arimathea
Born: May 13, 1792 , Senigallia, Italy *Died:* February 7, 1878, Vatican City *Born:* November 25, 1881, Sotto il Monte, Italy *Died:* June 3, 1963, Vatican City *Born:* September 26, 1897, Concesio, Lombardy, Italy *Died:* August 6, 1978, Vatican City *Born:* May 18, 1920, Wadowice, Poland *Died:* April 2, 2005, Vatican City	Saint Peter, Saint Soter, Saint Fabian, Saint Damasus, Saint Leo the Great, Saint Gregory the Great, Saint Nicholas I the Great, Saint Gregory VII, Saint Celestine V, Saint Pius X

By Your Holy Cross Melody

Words Catholic Sacred Tradition
Music Nancy Scimone 2006

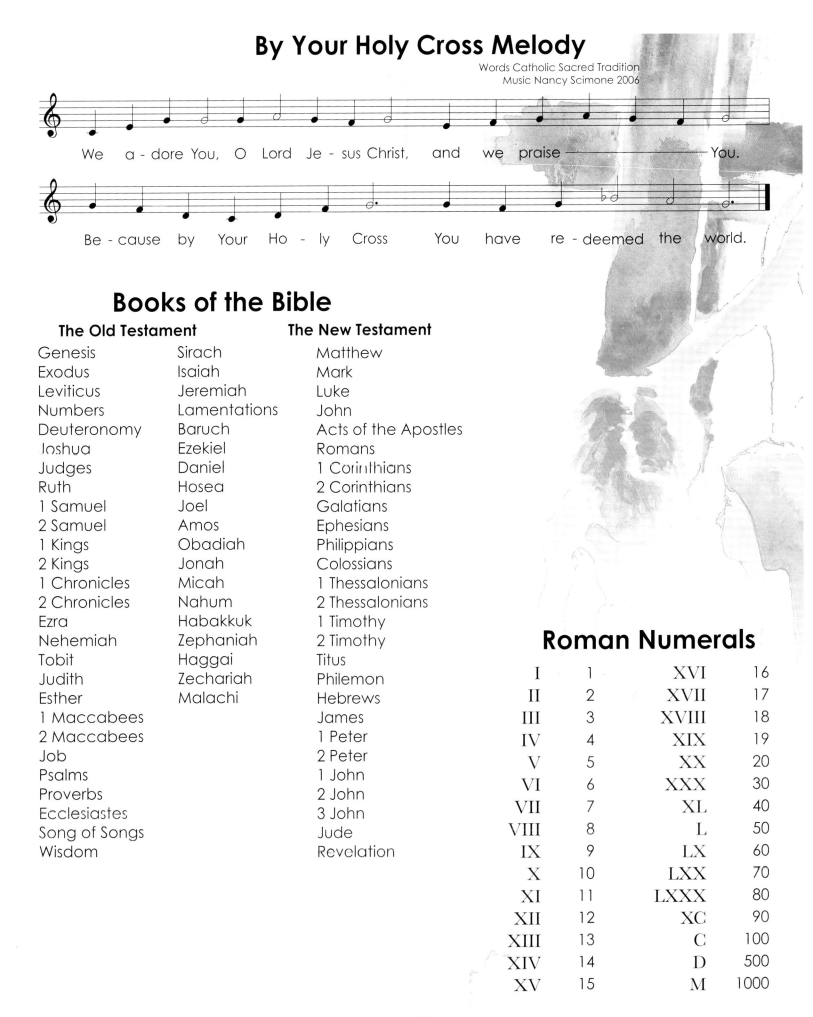

We a-dore You, O Lord Je-sus Christ, and we praise ——— You.

Be-cause by Your Ho-ly Cross You have re-deemed the world.

Books of the Bible

The Old Testament

Genesis	Sirach
Exodus	Isaiah
Leviticus	Jeremiah
Numbers	Lamentations
Deuteronomy	Baruch
Joshua	Ezekiel
Judges	Daniel
Ruth	Hosea
1 Samuel	Joel
2 Samuel	Amos
1 Kings	Obadiah
2 Kings	Jonah
1 Chronicles	Micah
2 Chronicles	Nahum
Ezra	Habakkuk
Nehemiah	Zephaniah
Tobit	Haggai
Judith	Zechariah
Esther	Malachi
1 Maccabees	
2 Maccabees	
Job	
Psalms	
Proverbs	
Ecclesiastes	
Song of Songs	
Wisdom	

The New Testament

Matthew
Mark
Luke
John
Acts of the Apostles
Romans
1 Corinthians
2 Corinthians
Galatians
Ephesians
Philippians
Colossians
1 Thessalonians
2 Thessalonians
1 Timothy
2 Timothy
Titus
Philemon
Hebrews
James
1 Peter
2 Peter
1 John
2 John
3 John
Jude
Revelation

Roman Numerals

I	1	XVI	16
II	2	XVII	17
III	3	XVIII	18
IV	4	XIX	19
V	5	XX	20
VI	6	XXX	30
VII	7	XL	40
VIII	8	L	50
IX	9	LX	60
X	10	LXX	70
XI	11	LXXX	80
XII	12	XC	90
XIII	13	C	100
XIV	14	D	500
XV	15	M	1000

Unit Study

Below are suggested ways to incorporate this book in teaching the importance of the Stations of the Cross, the Saints, the Devotions and the Papacy. The length of the assignment or activity should be adjusted to the student's age and ability.

The Stations of the Cross

• Research the history of the Stations of the Cross and identify those who were responsible for making this devotion part of the Catholic tradition. How does your parish carry on the tradition of the Stations of the Cross – during Lent, and other times of the year?

• Discuss the Gospel background for the Stations. (See the Study Matrix on page 38 for references.) Some Stations do not have explicit Gospel references. What are the implications for the lack of Gospel reference? Discuss the significance of tradition in the history of the Catholic Church.

• Take a pilgrimage to a Shrine. Use this prayer book as a guide for meditation and discussion while you walk the *Via Dolorosa*. Sing the meditations found on page 40.

• Traditionally, there are fourteen Stations of the Cross. Some churches have fifteen Stations, with the mystery of the Resurrection as the fifteenth. Discuss the significance and reason why some parishes have added this additional Station.

Saints

• With each Station is listed a Saint or Blessed who followed Jesus through a life of holiness. Select one of these holy men or women, research their life, and write a short biography. Illustrate the biography by creating a collage of significant events in their lives.

• Compare and contrast some of the saints. Who were the youngest and who were the oldest? Who were members of religious orders and who were laity? What religious orders did some of these holy men and women establish? Who were the richest and who were the poorest? In what countries were they born and did they remain in those countries or did they travel to other countries, perhaps to evangelize? What message did these holy men and women leave for our generation?

• What is the difference between a Saint and a Blessed?

• We are all called to sainthood and a life of holiness. Discuss how to reach that plateau but identify pitfalls and difficulties encountered through the media and peer pressure. Use examples from the list of Saints found on page 39 in the Study Matrix.

Devotions

• Discuss the role of devotions, such as, the Most Holy Rosary and the Stations of the Cross, in the life of a prayerful Catholic.

• Relate the similarities between the Stations of the Cross and the Most Holy Rosary. For additional information on the Most Holy Rosary, see Christine and Gus' first book, <u>Speak, Lord, I am Listening</u>.

• The Chaplet of Divine Mercy is a recent prayer devotion. For information on how to pray the Chaplet, see page 36. Discuss how the mystery of the Crucifixion and the mystery of Divine Mercy are related. How is the Divine Mercy message revealed in the Diary of Saint Maria Faustina? What is the significance of the 3 o'clock hour?

Papacy

• Jesus Christ founded the Catholic Church and through the succession of Popes, starting with Saint Peter, the papacy continues today with His Holiness Pope Francis. Discuss the lives of the four Popes listed on pages 33-35. Discuss how their efforts are continued from one to the next. Use examples, such as, the Second Vatican Council, the annual Message of Peace, and their Encyclicals.

Other Titles available from Suffering Servant Scriptorium
Prayer Books

Speak, Lord, I am Listening (2nd Ed, with Luminous Mysteries and Study and Discussion Guide) This prayer book presents the richness of the Sacred Mysteries of the Most Holy Rosary in terms that children can visualize and understand. Gus Muller's watercolors use the full palette of color expression to explore the depths of the agony of Christ crucified and reach the heights of the Blessed Virgin Mary's glorious reign as Queen of Heaven and Earth. Succinct and most apt meditation selections yield a wealth of spiritual insight into the mysterious events of the lives of Jesus and Mary. The Scriptures and watercolor illustrations coupled with the prayers of the Most Holy Rosary provide a rich meditation platform for teaching prayer and devotion to Jesus and Mary.

In His Presence This book of meditations outlines SEVEN VISITS to the Blessed Sacrament. This prayer book can be used in one evening, such as, during the Holy Thursday Seven Church Pilgrimage. It can be used for seven consecutive days for a special prayer request. And, it can be used periodically, whenever you can spend time visiting Jesus in the Blessed Sacrament. This prayer book includes illustrations from Dante's Divine Comedy from the inspired artistry of the 19th century Catholic illustrator Gusave Dóre.

Psalter of Jesus and Mary This pocket-size Scriptural Rosary prayer book includes the 150 Psalms Scriptural Rosary for the Joyful, Sorrowful and Glorious Mysteries and meditations for the Luminous Mysteries from the Book of Proverbs, the wise words of Solomon. The 20 Mysteries of the Most Holy Rosary open with a New Testament reflection. There is a short Scripture meditation from either Psalms or Proverbs for each Hail Mary. An Old and New Testament icon from Julius Schnorr von Carolsfeld's Treasury of Bible Illustrations accompany each mystery.

His Sorrowful Passion This prayer book integrates Sacred Scripture meditations with the prayers of the Chaplet of Divine Mercy. There are two Scriptural Chaplets: one chronicles Jesus' Passion and the other features the Seven Penitential Psalms. The woodcuts of the 15th century Catholic artist, Albrecht Durer, illustrate this book.

Sanctify my Heart Suffering has redemptive value when we recognize God's mighty Hand in the events and offer our day to Him. Accepting God's will in all suffering is a sacrificial prayer by sharing in the sacrifice at Calvary. Christine Haapala's tenth Scriptural prayer book encourages us to allow the Holy Spirit, the Sanctifier, to shape and mold our hearts into an imitation of the Sacred Heart of Jesus and the Immaculate Heart of Mary. Through reflective and meditative selections from Sacred Scripture, this daily journey is a call to conversion when we encounter the Theological Virtues, the Gifts of the Holy Spirit, and the Fruit of the Holy Spirit.

Seraphim and Cherubim A Scriptural Chaplet of the Holy Angels. Angels have been with us since the beginning in the "Garden of Eden" and will be with us at the "End of Age." This prayer book joins together Sacred Scripture selections with special invocations to our Blessed Mother and the Holy Archangels. This book includes fabulous full-color pictures from the masters, such as, Raphael, Bruegel the Elder, Perugino and many others.

Pearls of Peace Spiritually walk in Jesus' footsteps by praying the mysteries of the Most Holy Rosary and meditating on the accompanying Holy Land photography. Follow the Holy Family from Bethlehem to Nazareth to Jerusalem. Walk with Jesus, his Blessed Mother, and his disciples to places, such as, Cana, the Sea of Galilee, Mount of Temptation, Mount Tabor, Garden of Gethsemane, Via Dolorosa, and Calvary.

The Suffering Servant's Courage (2nd Ed, with Luminous Mysteries) This prayer book integrates poignant Sacred Scripture verses about courage and fortitude, the prayers of the Most Holy Rosary, and illustrations from the inspired artistry of the 19th century Catholic illustrator Gustave Dóre.

From Genesis to Revelation: Seven Scriptural Rosaries This prayer book is the most thorough and extensive collection of Scriptural Rosaries you will find anywhere. This prayer book goes well beyond the traditional Scriptural Rosary and penetrates the heart of the meditative spirit of the mysteries.

Recorded Prayers available on CD

The Sanctity of Life Scriptural Rosary (2nd Ed. with Luminous Mysteries) Sacred Scripture selections prayed with the Most Holy Rosary uniquely brings you God's message of the dignity and sanctity of life. The prayers are accompanied by meditative piano music. Four different readers lead you in more than two hours of prayerful meditations. Includes four songs from the composer and soprano Nancy Scimone, winner of the UNITY Awards 2002 Best Sacramental Album of the Year for ORA PRO NOBIS. Includes 16-page book with the complete text of the Sacred Scripture selections. Double CD. CD 1 includes the Joyful and Luminous Mysteries and CD 2 includes the Sorrowful and Glorious Mysteries.

Time for Mercy Composer and singer Nancy Scimone offers you a new, spiritually uplifting Chaplet of Divine Mercy melody. This Scriptural Chaplet of Divine Mercy is based on the Penitential Psalm Scriptural Chaplet of Divine Mercy from the book, His Sorrowful Passion. Brother Leonard Konopka, MIC, prays selections from the Seven Penitential Psalms, while Nancy Scimone's crystal clear soprano voice brings us God's message of Divine Mercy and Infinite Grace. The CD includes the meditation song, "Thy Heart Immaculate", which was inspired by Saint Faustina who wrote in her Diary that the Blessed Virgin Mary said "I am not only the Queen of Heaven, but also the Mother of Mercy." (Diary, 330)

To purchase additional copies of this book or the works mentioned above, please visit your local Catholic bookstore. Individual orders or quantity discounts are also available by calling us at 888-652-9494. For more detailed information about these products and Suffering Servant Scriptorium and to listen to selections of the music and prayers, please visit www.sufferingservant.com.